MW00883028

THE EGYPT OF
NEFERTITI

T.D. VAN BASTEN

TABLE OF CONTENTS

INTRODUCTION

For centuries, the beautiful, mysterious Queen Nefertiti, has captured our imaginations. We do not know very much about the woman's origins, or her demise, which only adds to her mysterious appeal. What we do know, however, is that she was the wife of one of the most controversial and radical of all of ancient Egypt's Pharaohs.

Her husband, Akhenaten, often referred to as the "Heretic King" started a revolution for the proto-monotheistic cult of Aten, the sun disk. This revolution led to dramatic social and political changes during what was later called the Amarna Period. From a huge upheaval in the traditional power structure of the nation, the outlaw of traditional gods, and even the relocation of the capital of the nation, there were actually deliberate attempts from the rulers who came after to erase this period of Egyptian history from the historical record. And they nearly succeeded.

What we do know about Nefertiti is that she was stunningly beautiful and incredibly powerful. She was, in fact, one of the most powerful queens in Egyptian history. Many scholars claim that she was the prime confidante, as well as advisor, to her husband during his reign. She is shown in a position of power in artistic depictions that is usually reserved for a king—whether she is shown smiting Egypt's enemies or even racing chariots or leading religious ceremonies.

Her level of influence and power was unprecedented for a woman in the ancient world. The background of Nefertiti is unknown, and many speculate a variety of possibilities of her origins from her being a mere peasant, to even being the Biblical Jezebel. We know she was highly intelligent and well versed in politics and religion and was incredibly close to her husband.

The little we know about her life is made even more exciting by the mystery surrounding her birth and death. Around year 14 in her husband's reign, Nefertiti literally disappears from the historical record. Much speculation surrounds her ultimate fate. Many theories abound, from the idea that she succumbed to plague, was exiled by her husband, or even lived on as a pharaoh herself, under a different identity.

New evidence found in King Tut's tomb may actually shed some proverbial light on these mysteries if, in fact, what lies behind the walls of Tut's tomb is the final resting place of the famously beautiful, mysterious Queen Nefertiti.

THE 18TH DYNASTY
1561 B.C. – 1323 B.C.

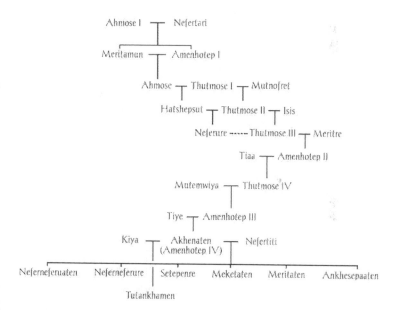

INTRODUCTION

I

NEFERTITI'S MYSTERIOUS ORIGINS

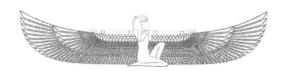

Aside from Cleopatra, there is no ancient Egyptian woman more well-known than Nefertiti. Though for all we think we know about her, there is still so much more that we haven't even discovered yet. History best knows her for her alleged beauty, as well as being the wife and co-ruler of the so-called "Heretic King," Akhenaten.

There are many speculations and alternative theories as to Nefertiti's origins. Some claim she was an exotic foreign beauty, others purport that she was an Egyptian peasant woman, whereas other have even more far-reaching claims about her linage, which will be discussed below.

Nefertiti means "the beautiful one has come" which definitely adds reinforcement to the idea that she was stunningly beautiful. This is also backed up by the iconic bust of Queen Nefertiti found in the early 1900s, that all of us equate with her.

Though there are different stories of her origins and how she met Amenhotep IV, who would later change his name to Akhenaten. One of the more popular stories states that they met and wed when she was just 15, before Akhenaten's ascent to the throne.

What is known for sure is that she became the Great Royal Wife and chief consort of one of the most controversial of all of Egypt's many Pharaohs. She would bear him six children, but there are no inscriptions or depictions of a son borne by Queen Nefertiti. She was also the step-mother of the famous Boy-King, King Tut.

In addition to portraying her as beautiful and stately, she is also often depicted with an elongated skull—a trait she shared with her husband Akhenaten. It is unknown as to how this cranial deformation came to be, especially since it was seen in both of them. Although, it has been said that they are considered to be relatives, at least cousins, as Ay was the brother of Akhenaten's mother. Some believe that the elongated skull was a result of a genetic anomaly, while others believe it was the result of head binding, which was a practice seen in many places throughout the ancient world.

Recent studies of her step-son's tomb have led to speculation of a possible additional chamber in the tomb. Some are speculating that these chambers might hold the remains of one of the most famous women of the ancient world.

1

Nefertiti means "the beautiful one has come" which definitely adds reinforcement to the idea that she was stunningly beautiful.

THE BIBLE'S JEZEBEL

One of the more colorful claims as to Nefertiti's lineage is that she is actually the Jezebel that is spoken of in the Old Testament of the Bible. There are historians that claim that there are similarities between the two life stories. There is speculation that Nefertiti may have been married previously. In the Old Testament, Jezebel is married to King Ahab of Israel, until his death, upon which she had to flee the Holy Land.

Some have gone so far as to speculate that Nefertiti was Jezebel, and that she even returned to Israel, as Jezebel did, in shame as she had failed to produce her new husband (in this case, Akhenaten) a son, the all-important male heir.

Jehu, who in the Bible ultimately slays Jezebel, is speculated to have been Horemheb. Horemheb was an official of the Egyptian dynasty and would succeed Ay to the throne. Ay is notable for becoming pharaoh after the death of King Tut, Nefertiti's step-son (and some speculate that Ay was her father or uncle, as previously stated). In fact, it was Horemheb who did the most to advance the campaign to erase the Heretic King and his family from the historical record through the destruction of inscriptions and monuments.

There are many problems with this theory, which has kept it from becoming widely accepted. First, there's a rough 500-year gap in the time line between the two women. Secondly, history notes that Jezebel was a strict follower of the goddess, Astarte.

As Nefertiti and her husband were proponents of one of the first monotheistic traditions that surrounded the worship of Aten, the Sun Disk, this doesn't really make sense with what we know about their rule.

NEFERTITI AS TADUKHIPA

Another theory surrounding the lineage of Nefertiti is that she may have been Tadukhipa, which was the daughter of King Tushratta and Queen Juni of Mitanni. Scholars who support this idea claim that this being true would help put some of the mysteries surrounding both of these women in order. If Nefertiti was, in fact, Tadukhipa, it would explain her seemingly unknown origins, as well as the ultimate fate of Tadukhipa, who seems to disappear fairly suddenly from the record.

Supporters of this theory argue that Tadukhipa's name was changed upon becoming the chief consort and Great Royal Wife to Akhenaten.

Unfortunately, due to time, and the deliberate attempt to erase the record of this time period, there is very little information that can be used to support or deny this theory of her lineage. In fact, there are also people who believe that Tadukhipa was, in fact, Kiya, who was one of Akhenaten's lesser wives.

NEFERTITI AND AY

The most commonly accepted and oft-cited lineage of Nefertiti is as the daughter of Ay, who would become pharaoh after the death of her step-son, the Boy-King Tut. One of the interesting things about this claim is that, like the other claims of her heritage, there is little to no evidence to support this theory. There are definitely links between Ay and the reign of Nefertiti, including close familial relations. However, there is not much to support her being his daughter.

This theory is largely based on a depiction of Queen Nefertiti and King Akhenaten giving his wife, Tiye, golden necklaces. This carving is found in Ay's burial tomb. However, other inscriptions directly state that Ay's wife, Tiye, was Nefertiti's wet nurse, not her mother. There are no direct relations between Tiye and Nefertiti outside the fact that she was her wet nurse that we know of, which does not lend much credibility to this theory.

Though there was obviously a relationship between the families, there is not much to indicate Ay and Tiye for her parentage. There are those who support the theory that Ay is her father, but note that she was borne by a lesser wife or concubine and that Tiye raised her as her own. There are others who speculate that Nefertiti was, perhaps, Ay's niece.

DAUGHTER OF AMENHOTEP III AND TEY

The last theory of Nefertiti's parentage that we will cover here is the idea that she was the daughter of Amenhotep III and his Great Royal Wife, Tey. These were also the parents of Amenhotep IV, who would later become known as Akhenaten. Though incest and sibling marriages were commonly seen in ancient Egypt, there is, again, not much evidence to support that this was the case. Though, it would do a lot to explain the allegedly elongated skulls of both Akhenaten and Nefertiti.

Still others state that it is possible that the queen and king were half-siblings. This indicates that Nefertiti was the child of Amenhotep III and a lesser wife or concubine. This is not readily accepted due to the lack of supporting evidence. Nowhere is Nefertiti ever referred to as the king's daughter, which would have been custom.

Famously, on June 9. 2003, Egyptologist Joann Fletcher, of the University of York, would claim that one of the female mummies found in the tomb referred to as KV35, in the Valley of the Kings, was none other than Nefertiti.

In 1898. Victor Loret found two female mummies, which he dubbed "the Elder Lady" and the "Younger Lady" while excavating the tomb of Amenhoptep II, The "Younger Lady" was also sometimes called "Lady X." Fletcher, on that fateful

[12]

day in 2003, claimed that she had determined that this was Nefertiti. It appears, though, that her claim was a bit rushed.

Later evidence shows that the "Younger Lady" was Akhenaten's biological sister, not Nefertiti—although, if it was the case that Nefertiti was Amenhotep III and Tey's daughter, then the "Younger Lady" could still be Nefertiti. DNA evidence also supports that the "Younger Lady" and Akhenaten had produced the famous King Tut, further reducing the likelihood that she is Nefertiti. There is no evidence in the historical record that Nefertiti ever bore a son, let alone was the mother of King Tut. However, there are investigators, such as the French Egyptologist Marc Gabolde, who believes that Nefertiti was indeed the mother of King Tut.

In addition to the Boy-King Tut, it is suspected that Akhenaten fathered another daughter, perhaps with his sister, called Smenkhare. This daughter is who would be heir to the throne. Though what became of her is unknown, there are some who speculate that Smenkhare was an alias for Nefertiti, and that she, in fact, was the successor. Though, the reasons for doing this are not at all clear. Some key motivation would seem to be necessary for this explanation to hold much water.

It is safe to say that there is a lot left to be known about the origins of this famous woman. Perhaps it is all the mystery that surrounds her that has continued to captivate our imagination and interest throughout the years.

2

The Temple of Queen Hatshepsut, located in the Valley of the Kings. Rumors are that the tomb referred to as KV35, may be from none other than Nefertiti.

II

THE RISE OF THE CULT OF ATEN

Ancient Egypt had long supported many different gods. These gods often started out as patron gods of a city or a region, and then were adopted into the overall pantheon of gods as the country began to unify. For hundreds of years before the reign of Nefertiti and Akhenaten, the aspects of the sun god, Amun, and Re (or Ra) were the most widely worshiped of the pantheon. As the kingdom united, the gods were merged to refer to the sun god in general, and was dubbed Amun-Re.

During the time of Akhenaten, dramatic religious changes swept across the lands. Temples dedicated to Amun-Re were defunded or shut down. The priests, and later, even the people, were expected to worship only the sun disk, Aten. Neither the people nor the priests were very fond of the notion of giving up their long-standing beliefs, which led to a significant amount of social strife and internal disputes.

From the evidence that we can now see left on temple inscriptions and pictorial depictions of Queen Nefertiti, she was fully supportive of her husband's shift to the one god focus. She is often depicted as being blessed by the rays of the sun disk, as well as worshiping and presenting offerings to the god. This art also makes it very clear that Nefertiti was no ordinary royal wife. She was more akin to a co-ruler.

In Egyptian art, the size of a figure is a product of their importance to the other figures in the picture. The larger the image, the more important the figure is and vice versa. In many depictions, Nefertiti is rendered the same size as Akhenaten, indicating her relatively equal position to the king. As noted above, she is also depicted making offerings to Aten, which is an act typically reserved for the priests and king himself.

In an effort to promote or show support for the new religious ideology, Nefertiti changed her name as well. She became Neferneferuaten-Nefertiti, or "the Aten is radiant of radiance for the beautiful one has come."

At the beginning of this transition, there is not much evidence to show that this ideology was forced upon the people, though the priestly class saw significant changes to their duties and level of power within Egyptian society. What we do see is that as Akhenaten's reign progressed, "gods" became "god" which always referred to Aten.

Later in his reign as he became more insistent that Aten was the supreme god, and then, the only god. He launched a campaign to try and eradicate any signs of the competing and primary cult of the time, Amun-Re. There is evidence that he began to defund, and then remove funding completely, from all temples dedicated to Amun. Taking money and power away from what was, at the time, an incredibly powerful and wealthy priestly class, led to chaos and a power vacuum among the priesthood as it was their closeness with, and knowledge of, Amun-Re that gave them power and legitimacy.

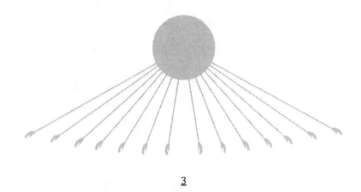

<u>3</u>

Aten refers to the sun disk with rays, which ends with hands, and was often thought of as another of the many different aspects of the sun god.

ATEN VERSUS AMUN-RE

When Akhenaten and Nefertiti took the throne, they had not yet begun the push for the transition to Aten as the supreme and only god. Akhenaten was born as Amenhotep IV and retained this name for the first five years of his kingship. In fact, it appears that he initially paid tribute to both aspects of the sun god: Aten and Amun-Re.

At the entrance of one of the temples to Re, Amenhotep/Akhenaten is shown worshiping Re. His enchantment with the incarnation of the sun god, Aten, was apparent early on. He commissioned the construction of a temple dedicated to Aten to be constructed in the holy city of Karnak, which was traditionally a place dedicated to the worship of Amun-Re.

For the priests and other supporters of the cult of Amun-Re, this departure from tradition had to be highly alarming, perhaps even upsetting. He oversaw a number of construction projects dedicated to Aten in the temple complex at Karnak. His personal Temple of Amenhotep IV, called Gempaaten (which means "the Aten found in the estate of the Aten"), was a huge construction of multiple buildings, which included a building dedicated to Nefertiti called the Hwt-Benben "Mansion of the BenBen stone."

We know of at least two other temples dedicated to Aten that were constructed in Karnak at that time: Rud-menu and Teri-menu.

Though there was an obvious preference for Aten, it does not appear that he withdrew support from the cult of Amun-Re during the first few years of his rule. Evidence even shows that the traditional place and level of power and influence was maintained by the High Priests of Amun, all the way through year 4 of Akhenaten's reign.

AMENHOTEP BECOMES AKHENATEN

Sometime in the fifth year of his reign, Amenhotep IV became Akhenaten. The circumstances leading up to this dramatic departure from tradition are not clear, but depart from tradition they did. Shortly after taking on the new moniker, Akhenaten set about establishing a new capital city for Egypt, replacing the traditional capital of Thebes (now Luxor), with the newly established Akhetaten, now referred to as Amarna.

Kings during this period had a five name titular that referred to the five different titles held by the king, who includes the Horus name, Nebty, Golden Horus name, Nomen, and Prenomen (also called the Nesu Bity). Upon his transition to Akhenaten, he had all but his Prenomen altered to show this change as well.

This era is often called the "Amarna Period" as it marks the short move of Egypt's traditional capital from Thebes to Akhetaten.

It should be noted that Aten was not a new god, but until the time of Akhenaten, Aten had not received a high level of worship or notice.

PRIESTLY POWER CHANGES

The priests of Amun had, over many hundreds of years, managed to carve out positions of tremendous wealth and power for themselves, becoming one of the upper classes of Egyptian society. Akhenaten's rule threatened this power, which was highly troubling to the priests who had little control or choice but to follow the orders of their king.

During the religious chaos of the Amarna Period, the priests of Amun were forced to change their allegiance and offer service to the cult of Aten. Many would reluctantly follow these orders, but bitterly. All who could secrete sacred objects and documents out of the temple to help ensure that they were not destroyed in the purge of references to Amun-Re in temples and state constructions. Priests who refused to change their allegiances were simply replaced by newly ordained priests of Aten.

It comes as no surprise that there was an intense and high level of animosity between Akhenaten and the priestly class.

THE POWER OF THE PRIESTS OF AMUN

It was during the reign of the famous female Pharaoh, Hatshepsut and, to an even greater extent, her successor, Thutmose III, that the cult and by default, the priesthood of Amun began to curry favor in the proverbial halls of power. From the time of Hatshepsut through Akhenaten, the priests of Amun were some of the most powerful and wealthy people in all of Egypt, forming a strong, influential upper class. The nature of his power, Akhenaten, came from his participation in designation of pharaohs by religious omens, which resulted at a later stage into obtaining power and wealth from the pharaohs.

The highest priests of Amun were based in the traditional capital city of Thebes where the four most-ranking priests served. These were the High Priest of Amun at Karnak, the Second Priest of Amun at Karnak, the Third Priest of Amun at Karnak, and the Fourth Priest of Amun at Karnak. These four, in addition to the High Priest of Amun at Thebes formed the upper echelons of the priestly power stricture at the time.

The king himself was in charge of selecting the High Priest of Amun at Thebes. The high priests also often held other positions of power and responsibility within the kingdom. Sometimes, a priest would even rise to the role of Vizier and later, even rule the country for a short period of time, such was their level of power in ancient Egypt.

In addition to the power vested in them by their religious stature, the priests of Amun also had a huge influence and power over the general economy of Egypt. The priests laid claim to their temples and the land that surrounded them. It is said that during the height of the power of the priests of the Amun, they controlled close to 2/3 of all temple lands in Egypt, some 90% of all her boats, and a significant portion of valuable resources as well.

The actual function and duties of the high priests of Amun are very different from what we think of as priestly duties today. These priests did not prepare and issue sermons, they did not disseminate religious teachings, or bring the gods to the people as today's priests do. Their job was to perform daily and festival rituals that the kingdom relied upon to ensure the continued functioning of the state. Their key job was to perform important daily rituals, oversee festival rituals, and to provide regular offerings to Amun-Re.

To the ancient Egyptians, the performance of these rituals were vital to ensure that Amun continued to look upon the Egyptian people with favor, as well as to ensure the continued continuity of life and the gods.

These priests often also functioned as scribes or key record keepers for their local Nome, or region. They also typically assisted in other administrative functions of government as well.

During festivals, the high priests also had very important roles to play, such as the oversight of the traditional processionals of altars or statuary between temples during important festivals.

There were also mystical elements associated with the high priests of Amun. They were tasked with understanding and explaining omens (which could be good or bad), as well as providing oracular services to the king and even the population at large. In some cases, the high priests also had the duty of interpreting dreams.

THE NATURE OF THE CULT OF ATEN

Before the time of Akhenaten, the sun god, Aten, was relatively unknown. We first see a mention of Aten during the 12th dynasty, but Aten would not play a significant role in religion or society until the time of the so-called Heretic King.

Aten refers to the sun disk and was often thought of as another of the many different aspects of the sun god. Until the "Amarna Heresy" as some call this time period, he was a minor god with no known major traditions or significant following. This was completely reversed during Akhenaten's reign, where Aten became first the supreme god, then the only accepted god.

There are many who equate the cult of Aten with nature worship. Many of the hymns, inscriptions, and rituals are based on the concept of nature being a beautiful and wondrous creation, which owed its existence to the all-important power of Aten, the sun disk, who is directly responsible for all life.

Another key departure from tradition during this unique period of Egyptian history is the notion that only the king and his family can connect with the gods. Aten was not available, directly, to the citizens of Egypt, but rather indirectly, through respect, worship, and observance of the king and his family.

In the "Great Hymn to the Aten," written by Akhenaten himself, Aten is credited as the creator of life, the creator of the world, and the means by which life is perpetuated. Aten embraces both masculinity, as well as the sacred feminine, united. This might be why Akhenaten is often depicted in an androgynous way that shows him bearing both masculine and feminine features.

Aten was not portrayed as a human or human-animal hybrid form, only as the sun disk with rays extending away from the disk.

In Atenism, as it is often called, there is a key balance between dark and light, but with distinct preference given to the light, associated with Aten. Amun became associated with the dark, particularly as the sun that visits the underworld in the evening. Darkness was almost seen as a scary, dangerous time, best to be avoided if possible. Work, worship, and rituals should take place during the day.

Due to his role as the closest embodiment of Aten on earth, Akhenaten himself had a divine quality. Worship of the king was as close as the regular people would get to communing with god. Akhenaten even took on roles that in ancient Egyptian mythology were performed by a number of specific gods, such as the judgment upon death which determines whether or not one will be rewarded entrance into the afterlife.

[27]

There were daily rituals performed at temples of Aten, but these were different than the rituals for the more traditional gods. The more traditional gods also had a human or human-animal hybrid embodiment. Temples held statues and altars to these gods which had to be fed, clothed, purified, and had offerings presented to them. As there is no physical embodiment of Aten, these rituals were unnecessary. There is, however, evidence of ritual incense burning performed several times a day in the temples to Aten.

There are those that argue that the Amarna period marks the first monotheistic religion, but this would only be partly true. In the beginning, other gods were noted and then thrown by the wayside upon the adoption of Aten as the only god. This made it very different from traditional monotheistic religions which do not ever acknowledge the existence of other gods.

It would be more correct to refer to the early period of Atenism as henotheism. This is the belief that one god is superior and the almighty god, but does not argue that other gods do not exist. Basically, they just say that Aten is the "top god." As time went on, Akhenaten got more extreme in his beliefs as well as governance of the country, turning it into what many historians refer to as a proto-monotheistic religion. It was during his 9th year of reign that this extreme transition took place, Aten becomes the sole accepted god, not just the supreme god of the pantheon.

III

The Heretic King Akhenaten

As noted in the previous chapter, Akhenaten was born as Amenhotep IV. He changed his name, and turned Egyptian society on its proverbial head, in the fifth year of his reign. It was at this time that Amenhotep became Akhenaten, and the revolution of the cult of Aten began in earnest. At first, this was the declaration of Aten as the supreme god and later, Aten as the only legitimate god—an early form of proto-monotheism. He continues to be one of the most mysterious and controversial figures in all of ancient Egypt for the dramatic changes he wrought on the very heart of Egyptian culture.

The 10th king of the 18th dynasty, his successors would do much to try to erase the so-called heretic king from the historical record. From the beginning, there were issues with his claim to the throne and the legitimacy of his rule. In fact,

Akhenaten was not raised as heir to the throne. It was actually supposed to be his brother that would take over as king upon their father's death, but Akhenaten's brother died before he could take the throne, leaving Akhenaten as the heir. Death was always close at hand in ancient Egypt, even royal bloodlines were not immune. The fact that there were so many different threats to a prolonged life goes far to explain the infatuation with death and the afterlife.

When Akhenaten took power, Egypt was at the height of its international power and influence. Egypt was, arguably, the wealthiest nation in the world at the time. When he died, the country was in turmoil and on the verge of collapse. Akhenaten was still a teenager when his father died, Akhenaten/Amenhotep ruled with his mother, Tiye, serving as co-regent until Akhenaten came of age. It was then that he ascended the throne in his own right.

His reign saw huge, dramatic shifts in the traditional power structure of Egyptian society; a different relationship between average citizen and god; a different level of power for the king and his family. Traditionally, the priestly class was the most powerful part of Egyptian society outside the king. As the reach of the cult of Aten spread—with its different relationship been god and the people—priests began to lose much of their power, influence, and even wealth. The king took their place in most aspects of religious life.

As a matter of fact, the revolution of Akhenaten seems to have arisen primarily in order to stop the growing power of the priests of Amun, which was immense when he came to power. Even his father, Amenhotep III, had already started to disassociate from the priests of Amun in order to stop their increasing power. Although, not by instituting a new cult, but by moving his residence away from Thebes.

Due to the motivated actions of later pharaohs, including his own son, the boy-king Tut, much of the so-called Amarna period was literally expunged from history. Horemheb, the Pharaoh that ruled after Ay, would spearhead a campaign to defile and destroy as many elements of the Amarna period as possible. The dramatic departure from tradition was highly unpopular, which resulted in even the short-lived capital of Amarna to be deliberately destroyed.

It was not until the French, under Napoleon, that this city would be rediscovered. Though there was mention of this city by a French priest, it was not until the time of Napoleon that the city would truly begin to reveal itself to the world in 1798. It is well-known that Napoleon was a huge fan of ancient Egypt and did much to bring the antiquities of the nation to the French people.

Even Napoleon did not fully unveil the extent of the city, its construction, and its incredible departure from tradition until the city was more fully mapped out in 1824. Subsequent excavation and documentation efforts started to reveal this contentious period to the world. Though subsequent rulers did much to try to erase Akhenaten and Nefertiti, they could not destroy them completely.

Once the revolution for the worship of Aten was underway, Akhenaten withdrew funding for cult temples dedicated to the traditional gods, particularly those dedicated to the god Amun. During this revolution, many temples, inscriptions, and works of art were systematically destroyed at Akhenaten's request.

THE FOUNDATION OF AKHETATEN

There is much about the dramatic shift from the traditional polytheistic pantheon of ancient Egyptian gods to Akhenaten's singular worship of the sun disk, Aten, which is lost to history and may never be known. Some historians claim that Akhenaten had a powerful vision, which, in turn, prompted the many major changes Egypt would see under his rule.

The legend states that he had a powerfully moving vision of the sun disk, Aten, perfectly centered between two mountains, shining down, as if giving him a message. He took this as a sign that he should pursue the spread of Atenism, and also build a city at the exact center between those mountains, dedicated to Aten.

This is how he determined where to locate his new capital city, Akhetaten, later known as Tell al-Amarna. Akhetaten means "Horizon of the Aten," which is in keeping with the legend about the origins of the city's location. Located about 250 miles south of Thebes (modern day Luxor), this quickly-erected city was abandoned shortly after the death of Akhenaten.

Unlike other historical and archaeological sites, Akhetaten was not a city lost to the ravages of sand and time. Quite the contrary, there is a lot of evidence that the city was intentionally destroyed. The ruins lay, reposed, ghostly, in the midst of a desert expanse. This is an indication to how much Akhenaten attempted to stray from tradition during his rule.

Akhetaten was necessary as a result of Akhenaten's vision and it would be a city solely dedicated to Aten, the sun disk and supreme god of the Egyptians. The city would boast many temples, as well as royal tombs, and a necropolis. He was in need of a new city, one that was not already steeped in the worship of other gods, and thus when he had his vision, he knew that he needed to establish a city solely dedicated to Aten, as well as the divine status of the royal family.

As with the temples to Aten seen in Thebes and at Karnak, these temples were open at the top to allow worshipers direct access to the sun during their ceremonies and rituals.

It is thought that the main part of the city construction was completed in less than five years, by the ninth year of his reign, showing this to be a dramatic architectural undertaking. The city was divided into three main sectors, separated by function. The North City was where the royal residences were located. The central area of the city was where most of the temples and administrative buildings were located. The so-called Southern Suburbs, comprising, obviously, the southern portion of the city, was where the bulk of the citizenry resided.

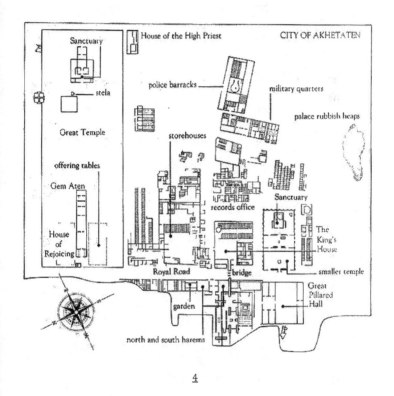

4

Akhenaten created a new capital city,
Akhetaten "Horizon of the Aten."

THE ADMINISTRATION OF EGYPT

There are many historians who claim that, overall, Akhenaten was a neglectful and ineffectual ruler, so focused he was on the spread of the cult of Aten and all the reforms and changes that this transition entailed. It is almost as though domestic and international politics were of no interest to him and it is thought that the entire country was pretty much overseen by scribes, with the exception of the new holy city of Akhetaten.

We now know that regardless of how ineffectual Akhenaten was as an administrator, there were factors that were out of his control that plagued Egypt during his rule. There is a lot of evidence to support the claim that during the reign of Akhenaten, there was a deadly epidemic raging through Egypt and around the Middle East. Some have speculated that it was the Plague, others that it might have been the world's first known influenza epidemic.

Regardless of what caused the epidemic, because of the king's semi-divine status, the Egyptian populace seemed to take this as a sign that their gods were not pleased with the current way of things. There are some who argue that this association with Akhenaten's reforms and the ills that befell Egypt at the time also helps explain the fast, thorough destruction of his capital city. It is well known that the traditional pantheon of gods was quickly readopted after his death.

The famous Amarna Tablets also serve as corroborating evidence that Akhenaten neglected many aspects of his kingly duties during his rule. These tablets consist of administrative documents and correspondence, as well as communications from Egypt's imperial territory and allied rulers.

These letters complain of neglect so bad as to lead to social disorder and chaos. There were many allied kings that wrote, begging for gold, to help their ailing economies or assist in their needs for military forces. In addition to widespread consequences for the allies and outposts of Egypt, the Egyptian economy suffered significantly due to this neglect as well.

For allies and trade partners reliant on Egyptian gold and military support to secure their trade networks, these elements were critical and imperative to the functioning of their economy. When that support no longer came, the trade routes were quickly broken up. This not only had profound effects on Egypt's economy, but those of the trading nations as well.

So little seems to have been paid to international affairs, Egypt lost a good deal of its land holdings in Syria during Akhenaten's reign to the Hittites.

ART IN THE AMARNA PERIOD

The style of art seen during the reign of Akhenaten and Nefertiti was also a dramatic departure from traditional Egyptian custom. So much different that many historians have dubbed the art of this time "Amarna Art," or simply refer to it as the "Amarna Style." While so many aspects of this period of Egyptian history were intentionally destroyed, some of the elements of this unique artistic style were retained by later pharaohs.

Unlike the stoic, unmoving, formal depictions traditional to the art of ancient Egypt, art in the Amarna period was much more fluid. Figures were shown in motion. They were shown in raucous, crowd-filled scenes, as well as in intimate and informal interactions. All of these things were dramatically different from the stylized, formal, sparse nature of the traditional art of Egypt.

It is said that the art of this period is less formal, less stylized, and more in keeping with reality. The very content of the scenes was a dramatic departure from the traditional art that usually showed the king and his family in a religious, formal, or military context, not in private, intimate moments. Under Akhenaten, this changed. Much of the art of the period shows the king and his family in a caring, loving light.

The bodies in Amarna Art were not stylized to perfection. In traditional Egyptian art, both men and women are shown in a perfected, almost-formulaic manner. That is, the representations were often as the king wanted to be seen, not how he actually looked like. The kings were generally depicted with broad shoulders, narrow waists, muscled to perfection. The women were slender, with shapely breasts and a small stature.

However, the art of the Amarna period was very much different from this. The figures were shown with belly pudge, wrinkles, and imperfections. Akhenaten himself is almost always shown with a belly bulge, as well as rounded feminine hips and other exaggerated feminine features. The family of Akhenaten is almost always depicted with odd, elongated heads, still very much a mystery.

The figures were always depicted in the profile, which *was* in keeping with traditional Egyptian art.

As noted in an earlier chapter, the sun disk, Aten, was never given an anthropomorphic depiction. It was always shown as the sun disk with rays of light extending from it. These rays sometimes end in hands. There are many depictions of the king, queen, and their family being blessed by the sacred rays of the Aten.

The art of this period showed people depicted more realistically, flaws and all. The king and his family were also portrayed in a more human sense, as loving partners, parents, and normal human beings.

While so much of this time period was abandoned mere years after Akhenaten's death in year 17 of his reign, some elements of the revolutionary changes that he and Nefertiti brought to the lands of Egypt would not be thrown by the wayside, covered up, or destroyed. The art of the period is, perhaps, the most successful element of the rule of Akhenaten and Nefertiti, as this is the one thing that seemed to have a lasting influence on the country.

Though it is true that, after Akhenaten and Nefertiti, much of the art was, again, more traditional and stylized, there are certain elements that were retained from the Amarna style which would forever alter the way people were depicted in ancient Egypt. After this period, the art was more naturalized. Scenes were not just sparse, stylized depictions, there was life in the art, a human element, a uniqueness that was not achieved with the earlier formulaic style of art.

IV

AN OUTSTANDING WOMAN

It appears that from the very beginning of her husband's rule, Nefertiti was a highly valued ally with much more power than is traditionally given to even Great Royal Wives. She was his favorite sounding board and it is alleged that he discussed most, if not all, important decisions with her. This means she had unprecedented access and power for a wife in ancient times.

No other woman before her, outside of Hatshepsut and Sobekneferu, wielded the amount of power that Nefertiti did. The art and inscriptions of the time support the idea that she was an incredibly powerful queen that was amongst the most powerful women in ancient history.

There are depictions of Nefertiti on the same scale as her husband, the king. As noted in an earlier chapter, the scale of the person's image in reference to the other figures is indicative of their level of power and influence. In almost all depictions of Nefertiti, she is shown as just as large as her husband. There is artwork showing her smiting enemies, even wearing the blue warrior crown—an incredible departure from tradition.

It seems that she assisted Akhenaten with all aspects of the rule of Egypt. She and Akhenaten co-performed important religious and social rituals, ceremonies, and other events. It is thought that Nefertiti and Akhenaten had an incredibly close relationship, which much of the art and inscriptions of the time back up.

<u>5</u>

King Akhenaten and Queen Nefertiti illustrated on the same scale. The scale of the person's image in reference to the other figures is indicative of their level of power and influence.

HER LEGENDARY BEAUTY AND SKILLS AS A MOTHER

One of the most widely held beliefs about Nefertiti is that of her stunning beauty. This belief is due, in large part, to the discovery of the famous Bust of Nefertiti, excavated from the studio of the sculptor Thutmose. Discovered in 1912 by German Ludwig Borchardt, this is perhaps the most well-known bust of the ancient world and is now housed in the Neues Museum in Berlin, Germany.

In this bust, Nefertiti is depicted as long, slender, graceful, and regal. Her beauty still speaks to us many thousands of years later, it's as those she is timeless.

In almost all her depictions, she is shown as a graceful, beautiful woman. Her beauty is said to have been known worldwide. Even her name "the beautiful one has come" supports the notion that she was a woman of legendary beauty. There are some who have attempted to claim that she many not have, in fact, been as beautiful as she has been depicted.

There isn't much evidence to support this claim and very much evidence to the contrary so the idea of Nefertiti with an almost goddess-like beauty has stood the test of time.

There are many historians who claim that Nefertiti was also a caring, loving mother. This wasn't necessarily the tradition of the time. Queens often had wet nurses and a variety of staff that could, if she wanted, take care of all the functions a mother would normally provide.

However, if we are to go by the reliefs and other art that history has left us, Nefertiti was a caring, doting mother to her six daughters. She is shown as maternal, caring, and close to her children. Though she was unable to provide Akhenaten with a male heir, it does not appear that this caused undue strain on their relationship.

Akhenaten did produce a male heir, with a lesser wife, called Kiye. This child would later become one of the most famous Pharaohs in all of ancient Egypt, King Tut. As was custom, Tut did not remain with Kiye. He was brought to the royal palace where he could be raised with the family, as one of their own. Nefertiti, who would have been his step-mother (though some have argued otherwise, there is no real compelling evidence that Nefertiti was Tut's birth mother), raised his as her own and helped prepare him to be the next ruler of Egypt upon the death of his father.

The art from the time depicts Nefertiti as a much more maternal queen, often shown caring for or showing affection to her children. Many of the works of art at the time are of her, the king, and their children in everyday, intimate family scenes.

Whether this was just a type of propaganda, or an attempt to spread a desired image of the woman is unknown.

6

The famous Bust of Nefertiti, excavated from the studio of the sculptor Thutmose is now housed in the Neues Museum in Berlin, Germany.

MORE THAN JUST A ROYAL WIFE

There is a wealth of evidence that supports the idea that Nefertiti was far more than just a simple royal wife. Most of this evidence is found in the *talatats* or stone blocks in the Aten temples of Karnak and in Akhetaten (now referred to as Amarna). In many ways, it can be said that she acted as co-ruler, she was that influential and powerful during her life. Akhenaten is said to have relied heavily on her opinion and ideas in pretty much all areas of governance and administrative. This is a type of power for a woman that is almost unheard of in the ancient world.

Many historians point to the many artistic depictions of Nefertiti as evidence of her great stature and power. As described before, in Egyptian art, scale and size are directly related to the level of power the person displayed has (relative to the others shown in the image). Nefertiti is always shown large, equal in size to that of Akhenaten, the king. This shows that she was seen as just as powerful as the king himself.

Many of the activities that she is portrayed undertaking are also key pieces of evidence to the extent of her power. She is shown leading activities typically only led by the king. She is shown performing important religious rituals and leading celebrations, something that is almost unheard of in all of ancient history, not just that of Egypt.

She is shown wearing the blue royal warrior crown while smiting enemies in battle, meaning, she is shown as fighting in war. There are also images of her racing chariots with her husband and her performing activities alone that were generally only undertaken by people of great power.

She was invaluable in helping to launch and spread their new cult of Aten as is portrayed in the found evidence. Even Akhenaten was placed on records with his own words about the equality between him and his wife Nefertiti, particularly in their role in Atenism, as is shown in a boundary stela in Amarna. It is here where he said the following, referring to the foundation of Akhetaten:

"So make Akhet-Aten as an estate of the Aten, my father, in its entirety, for I have made it as a memorial, whether belonging to my name or belonging to her name—namely the Great Royal wife Neferneferuaten—Nefertiti—or belonging to his name forever and ever."

There is a lot of speculation, but unfortunately not a lot of evidence, that she may have ruled Egypt solely after Akhenaten's death, under an assumed name. There is the so-called Coregency Stela found in a tomb in Amarna, which is used as evidence of the co-regency role of Nefertiti, and even her possible role as successor of Akhenaten.

While we don't know how closely she played a role in actual administration, and certainly whether or not she served as sole ruler after the king's death, we do know that she was an independent woman who was granted an unprecedented level of power and influence for a woman in the ancient world. It is this, along with her beauty that continues to captivate so many people to this day.

V

HER FINAL DESTINY

For some reason, after year 14 of Akhenaten's 17-year rule, Nefertiti seemingly disappears from the historical record. One interesting thing to note is that around the same time she disappeared, it is documented that one of her daughter's, Mekitaten, died during child birth. Additionally, three other daughters of Nefertiti and Akhenaten are no longer referred to after this time and many scholars presume they died.

Some argue that this was, too, likely the fate of the famous Queen Nefertiti. However, she was a very powerful and influential woman, and the processes surrounding death and the ascent to the afterlife were incredibly important concepts to ancient Egyptians, so it is hard to believe that there would be no record of her death or journey to the afterlife.

There are some scholars who argue that due to the fact that she was unable to bear a male heir, or perhaps she backed away from the cult of Aten, and Akhenaten exiled her to retirement in one of the royal palaces, or perhaps even out of Egypt entirely. Again, there is not much evidence to support this theory.

Still others claim that she did, in fact, live on, perhaps, even, after the death of her husband Akhenaten. They speculate that she may have even ruled as sole pharaoh under a different name and even identity after the death of her husband.

ALTERNATE THEORIES

The fact that such a famous woman's death is shrouded in so much mystery goes far to explain why so many different theories as to her ultimate fate abound. We simply do not know what happened to her and, naturally, we want an explanation that fits what we know about history.

Exciting recent discoveries, to be discussed in more detail later in the chapter, may actually shed some light on these long-standing mysteries, but for now, all we have are the different theories. If we ever do, in fact, find her tomb and/or mummy, many historical mysteries could finally be solved.

Since we do not, as of yet, know her ultimate fate with any certainty, let's take a look at some of the different possible explanations for her disappearance from history.

Some say that she simply died, perhaps as a result of the plague or influenza outbreak that was ravaging Egypt and the Middle East at the time. While this is a reasonable explanation and it does make a lot of sense, the fact that there is no record of her illness, death, or burial, make it hard for people to accept this explanation as to her final fate.

An old-standing theory, popular with some of the earlier Egyptologists was that Akhenaten had her exiled in disgrace—perhaps she rejected the cult of Aten, or perhaps because she was unable to produce a male heir. However, again, what we do know about history does not support this. We know Akhenaten had sons with lesser wives and there is no indication that this ever posed an issue. Nefertiti also did so much to help expand and spread the cult of Aten, that it is hard to believe that she would have turned her back on it. Later historical finds, such as the tomb of King Tut, have caused this explanation to fall out of favor.

A small group of people support the notion that Nefertiti actually committed suicide as a result of grief over the death of Mekitaten in child birth. As with the other theories, it would seem that, since we know of the death of the daughter, we would know that Nefertiti took her life out of anguish.

One of the more popular theories is that she actually didn't die in the 14th year of Akhenaten's reign. Some claim that not only did Nefertiti live on, she actually went on to rule the country solely, under a different name and possibly identity. Part of the reason this theory has gained so much popularity is that we do not know the true identity of the pharaohs between Akhenaten and King Tut and there is the problem of her disappearance to attend to.

NEFERTITI BECOMES
NEFERNEFERUATEN

The period between the death of Akhenaten and the rule of his son, King Tut, is also mired in mystery. There are two individuals who are suspected to have had short periods of rule during this time, including an unknown female called Neferneferuaten. There are some historians and Egyptologists who claim that Neferneferuaten is none other than Nefertiti herself, but under a different alias.

What circumstances would have led to this outcome is hard to imagine, but there is a lot of mystery that surrounds the identity of this alleged female pharaoh who may have ruled for two short years. As noted above, there are those who believe this woman to have been Nefertiti, and others who claim that this was Nefertiti's daughter, Meritaten.

Part of the reason that this explanation is pleasing is that it would explain the relatively sudden appearance of Neferneferuaten, as well as the disappearance of Nefertiti. Supporters of this theory further speculate that, as Neferneferuaten, Nefertiti served as co-regent to Akhenaten before taking over the throne upon his death.

THE MYSTERIOUS LEADER
SMENKHKARE

Smenkhkare is another mysterious leader who was also said to rule in the short period between the death of Akhenaten and the rise of the boy-king Tut. What we do know about Smenkhkare is that his or her reign was quite short-lived and history does not provide us with any detail as to what happened during this time.

Like Neferneferuaten, it is speculated that Smenkhkare may have served as co-regent with Akhenaten in the final years of his life and rule, before ascending to the throne upon his death.

Some believe that, though historically portrayed as a male, Smenkhkare may have actually been Nefertiti. There is also speculation that Neferneferuaten and Smenkhkare are two different names for the same individual, further bolstering the claim that they were Nefertiti under a different name.

Part of the evidence that historians point to in support of the Nefertiti as Neferneferuaten/Smenkhkare theory is the coronation name of these later rulers. This is, typically, a unique name given only to one individual, and yet, this coronation name is shared by both Neferneferuaten and Smenkhkare, and is also the name that Nefertiti took upon her husband's transition from Amenhotep to Akhenaten.

NEFERTITI'S TOMB

Like her birth and death, the final resting place of Nefertiti is also a mystery. Though there have been many claims to have found the location of her tomb or remains, none have produced compelling evidence that has stood the test of time. To this day, the final location of this famous queen's tomb and mummy are still unknown. However, some recent archaeological finds may provide concrete evidence to some of the mysteries surrounding this famous woman.

In 2015, English archaeologist Nicholas Reeves performed a high resolution scan of King Tut's burial chambers. During this scan, he stumbled upon compelling evidence that there may be additional, as-yet-undiscovered, chambers within the tomb. In November of this year, the chamber was scanned using infrared thermography, which can show temperature fluctuations between surfaces. Large differences in temperature can indicate the presence of empty space behind a solid surface.

The evidence of both of these scans is that there is something behind these potential doorways. Due to the mystery surrounding her tomb, her connection to Tut, and the oddities surrounding the Tut burial, many are speculating that behind the walls may house the long-hidden tomb of one of the most famous women in the entire ancient world.

As of this time, researchers are now looking into how they may go about accessing these possible chambers safely. If there are rooms behind these walls, they have been hidden and left unexposed for some 3,500 years and are a part of one of the most important archaeological sites in all of ancient Egypt. The excavation must be done in a way that does not disturb what lies on either side of the wall.

The next few months are sure to hold some potentially exciting discoveries. These may, in fact, allow us to solve some of the mysteries of the ancient world. We can only hope that, if Nefertiti does lie behind these walls, that we can finally start to unravel some of the mystery that surrounds this woman and her contentious rule.

FALSE CLAIMS AND ZAHI HAWASS

As noted earlier, there have been many, short-lived, yet fevered periods where archaeologists or Egyptologists have thought they found, definitively, the remains or tomb of one of the most famous of all of Egypt's claims. Perhaps the most notable "false find" was made by a female Egyptologist in the early 2000s.

Joann Fletcher was granted unprecedented access to the tomb referred to as KV35 where, in 1912, three mummified bodies were found in an excavation. Two of these mummies appeared to be female and were dubbed as "the Elder Lady" and "the Younger Lady." Fletcher called the Younger Lady, "Lady X."

First, she was given permission to actually enter the tomb, referred to as KV35, something that almost no researchers are granted permission to do. According to Fletcher, much of her research had indicated that the mummy in tomb KV35 might actually be the remains of the famous Queen Nefertiti. She based this on many things, including the obvious royal nature of the burial, as well as the physical structure of the body, and analysis that showed embalming processes consistent to what we know was used during the time of Nefertiti.

To her good fortune, she was granted further access to the tomb. She was allowed to bring in a crew and high tech equipment to more fully examine the mummy of the so-called Lady X. Again, circumstantial evidence further convinced her that she had found Nefertiti, but not everyone was convinced. There was contradictory evidence in the subsequent analysis, some indicating the woman was much younger than we know Nefertiti could have been at her death, and others that are consistent with a woman of Nefertiti's suspected age.

Fletcher even went so far as to bring in forensic facial reconstruction experts to attempt to put a "face" to the mummy. She did this with the fanfare of a camera crew and a feature-length documentary about the alleged discovery. All of this would only further convince Fletcher of her landmark find.

Unfortunately for her, it was not Nefertiti and her dramatic claims would eventually lead to her being banned from doing more research in the country from one of the most controversial figures in all of Egyptology, Zahi Hawass. One thing she was right about was that Lady X was most definitely a royal figure. Later evidence shows that it is likely the remains of one of Akhenaten's sisters, or even a lesser wife. Some have speculated that it might be Kiya, the mother of Tut, but there isn't much to support this claim.

Though this was a very high profile example of a false claim, it was not, by any means, the only one. It was just hyped and promoted, then dramatically dis-confirmed.

Former Antiquities Minister and controversial Egyptologist, Zahi Hawass, is the bane of many researchers' proverbial side. From controversy surrounding his ethics and associations, to his outright attempts to stop further study and research, his tenure in the Egyptology community has been incredibly controversial and polarizing. One thing can be said about Hawass, he did bring much attention to the history of ancient Egypt and did much to improve security, archaeological practices, and also further the careers of more Egyptian Egyptologists, as it had long been a field dominated by Europeans.

It should be noted that Hawass has come out against Reeves' claims of finding additional chambers. He states that these speculations are unfounded and will fall by the wayside, but has yet to provide any reason as to why he believes this.

Hawass has long been mired in controversy. From claims that he smuggled priceless antiquities, banned researchers from continuing work, and even stole the discoveries of others, he's a very polarizing individual. Most people either love him or hate him and he has a direct connection to the attempts to locate and identify the remains of Queen Nefertiti.

When Fletcher came out with her dramatic claim that she had found the infamous Queen Nefertiti's remains in the tomb of KV35, Hawass was furious. She had been granted unprecedented access to this tomb and, his opinion, was making highly inflammatory and unfounded claims as to the identity of Lady X. So strong was his contempt and anger for her bold assertion, he later banned Fletcher from doing any further research in the country.

Later, DNA testing in 2010 showed, once and for all, that neither of these mummies was Nefertiti. Although, some scholars and stakeholders are still not giving all credit to these results and even propose alternative and forced theories. Such as the proposed one by the French Egyptologist Marc Gabolde, who mentioned that the DNA results can have a different interpretation, because of the incestuous behavior of Egyptian rulers, and so, a DNA result of brothers could be interpreted as one of cousin-brothers product of the blood ties through generations. In this case, this makes him still believe that Nefertiti could be King Tut's mom.

CONCLUSION

Mysterious, beautiful, and powerful, there is much lore that surrounds the life and death of one of ancient Egypt's most famous queens. From her mysterious origins to her unprecedented power, there is much about her to intrigue us, as well as make us ask questions.

She was the wife of one of the most controversial rulers in the history of ancient Egypt. She helped him spread the proto-monotheistic cult of Aten and destroy the worship of the traditional gods. These revolutionary changes caused such political and social turmoil that later generation sought to erase this entire period from the record, including the complete destruction of the short-lived capital, Akhetaten.

The level of her power is not entirely known, but we have strong evidence from inscriptions, documentation, as well as artistic portrayal, that she was afforded almost as much power as the king himself, something that was almost unheard of in the ancient world.

In addition to her power is the legend of her beauty and the mystery of where she came from and what happened to her. Like she seemingly came out of nowhere, she disappeared just as suddenly as well, leaving many to come up with sensational explanations as to her ultimate fate. The mystery, the allure of the unknown, drama, and intrigue are all integral parts of her story, and are also elements that capture the human imagination.

What we do know is that she was a beautiful, powerful wife and mother who lived during a time of religious upheaval and dramatic social change. Pretty much everything, including the art of this period, was completely unique and not in keeping with what was traditionally Egyptian. The society she ruled did much to destroy any vestiges of her and her husband's reign. While she was beautiful and charismatic, she and her husband oversaw one of the most contentious and least popular of ancient Egypt's Pharaohs. She may have had a mighty presence, but some changes are too dramatic and the priests and people of Egypt wanted to maintain the traditional gods.

We also know that these reforms were, perhaps, too dramatic for the people, as after their reign, Egypt quickly reverted to their traditional gods and returned to the traditional capital city. Later pharaohs actively worked to erase all traces of this period, known as the Amarna Period, all of which only adds to the element of intrigue and mystery surrounding this timeless queen.

A NOTE FROM T.D. VAN BASTEN

Thank you very much for reading The Egypt of Nefertiti, If you enjoyed it and found what you were looking for, please be so kind to take a moment to leave a review at your favourite retailer such as Amazon.

−T.D. van Basten

THE EGYPT OF NEFERTITI

ABOUT THE AUTHOR

Losing sense of time through television and technology, many seem to have forgotten about our ancestors and how the world has been shaped to what it is today. T.D. van Basten has set the tone for historical coverage and is admired by many for his exceptional passion, vivid descriptions and storytelling.

THE EGYPT OF NEFERTITI

ANCIENT EGYPT BIOGRAPHIES

THE EGYPT OF CLEOPATRA

Cleopatra VII (69 BC - 30 BC), the last Pharaoh of Egypt, was a very educated, crafty, ambitious and clever woman. Her intellect and charisma—far greater than her beauty and sexuality—allowed her to keep the power for nearly twenty years by fighting against—and allying with—the greatest power at the time, Rome. Although her history was written by who defeated her and, therefore, modified according conveniences of them, there have been found, in recent archaeology researches, evidences of her intellect and achievements that portrayed her beyond her beauty and sexual power. She captivated the two greatest Romans of her time, and destroyed herself. Cleopatra was representing everything that the Romans didn't like. Not only was she a woman, but she was a woman with power.

The Egypt of King Tut

Upon the opening of the famous tomb of King Tutankhamen, Carter and his team found a huge array of sumptuous grave goods. However, they also found a very small tomb, lacking the well-known royal depictions and wide array of different paintings and inscriptions. Even the grave goods, while luxurious, did not seem fit for a king for his journey to the afterlife.

The many mysteries surrounding Tut led to many fantastic rumors, including that of a curse on the tomb of the boy-king. Circumstances and seemingly sudden deaths, fueled by media coverage, helped ignite the rumor that there was a curse on the tomb and that those who worked within it or benefited from the goods within it would suffer a grisly fate. There were just enough bizarre coincidences to fuel the rumors and convince many of the existence of a curse on the tomb of King Tut.

The Egypt of Hatshepsut

Hatshepsut was arguably the most powerful female to rule as pharaoh during its long and storied history in the wealthy Egypt of the New Kingdom. Her rule was highly unconventional, yet she had the support of the power brokers at the time. Somehow, during her long reign as pharaoh with her stepson, she managed to maintain positive relationships with the right constituency, as well as her co-ruler. It would seem likely that, if there was internal strife within the royal house as to the moves made by Hatshepsut, there would be some documentation or indication of this tension in the historical record. As of the time of this writing, no evidence of poor relations or civil strife has ever been found.

THE EGYPT OF THUTMOSE III

Thutmose III was one of the most known and respected of all of Egypt's pharaohs, regardless of dynasty or time period. He ruled during the New Kingdom, which is often seen as the "star-studded" dynasty in ancient Egyptian history because that's the dynasty where many of the "big names" come from. He had the benefit of a lengthy co-rule that allowed him to develop and hone his military skills which would serve him incredibly well during his time in power.

His early life and rule were rather unusual, and he was a powerful person, even when he was just a mere infant. He was the son of Thutmose II and one of his lesser wives of common heritage. Thutmose II was married to the incredibly powerful Queen Hatshepsut, but the two were unable to produce a male heir which meant they had to look to Thutmose II's harem for a suitable successor. Thutmose III was the chosen successor.